Plastics

Terry Cash

Photographs by Ed Barber

Contents

How do you use plastics?   2
Collecting and sorting plastics   4
Testing plastics   6
From oil to plastics   8
How bags are made   9
Making moulds   10
How bottles are made   11
How buckets are made   12
New plastics from old   16
How egg boxes are made   17
How pipes and tubes are made   18
Plastics for clothes   20
How strong are plastics?   21
Do plastics keep things warm?   22
Plastics and the environment   24
More things to do   25
Index   25

A&C Black · London

How do you use plastics?

Almost everything that you use has some plastic in it.

Collecting and sorting plastics

How many different kinds of plastic can you collect?

Some plastic things, such as saucepan handles, are tough and strong. Others, such as food wrappers or carrier bags, are thin and papery.

Many plastics are brightly coloured, but some are white or even see-through. Some plastics, such as nylon, can be made into threads and woven into the material for clothes.

How will you sort out your collection? Into groups like this?

How many other ways of sorting and grouping can you find?

Testing plastics

Different kinds of plastic have different jobs to do. You could do some simple tests to find out more about the plastics in your collection.

Try bending the plastic. Does it bend ▶ easily or is it very difficult to make it change shape? Saucepan handles wouldn't be much use if they were made out of the soft, bendy plastic used for washing-up liquid bottles.

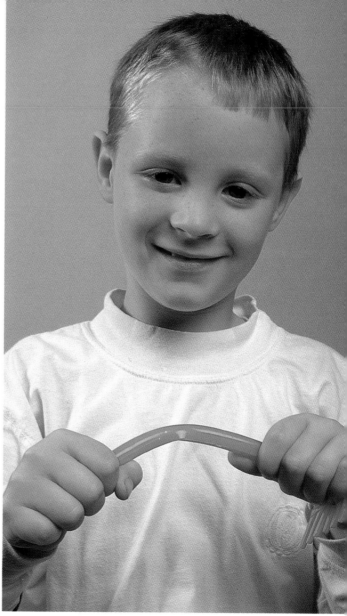

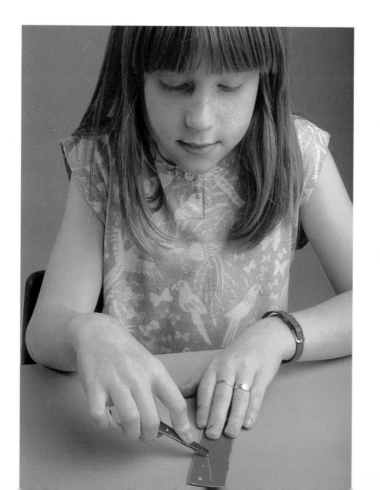

◀ Try scratching the plastic with your thumb nail. If this doesn't work, try using a pair of scissors. Soft plastics will mark quite easily; some are much harder. If plastic table tops or the lenses of glasses scratched easily, they would be spoilt very quickly.

How many of the things in your collection will float on water? Fill a large bowl or tank with water and put your plastic objects into the water one at a time. Before you put each object into the water, see if you can guess whether it will float or sink.

Will an empty plastic bottle float? Do you think a bottle full of water will float?

From oil to plastics

Most plastics are made from chemicals which come from oil. Each sort of plastic (such as nylon or polythene) is made from different chemicals. A chemical factory turns the oil into plastic granules, like the ones round the edge of this page.

Most plastics have no colour of their own so coloured dyes are added. Can you see the pieces of blue dye mixed in with these white plastic granules?

The plastic granules are delivered to factories which make products, such as bottles or bags. There are lots of different ways of making plastic products but they all have one thing in common. The plastic is heated until it goes soft and runny, like treacle. Then it can be made into different shapes. When the plastic cools down, it sets and keeps its new shape.

Some plastics can only be shaped once, but others can change their shape if they are heated again.

How bags are made

Bags are made from plastic that has been heated and rolled into thin sheets by machines with big, heavy metal rollers.

It's just like rolling out modelling clay or pastry with a rolling pin. Can you roll out a sheet of clay as thin as a plastic bag?

Making moulds

Most plastic things are shaped inside moulds. The mould is made to look like the outside of the product.

1. This is the mould for a toy boat.

2. The soft plastic is poured into the mould. When the plastic cools, it takes on the shape of the boat.

Would you like to try making your own mould?

You will need

An old spoon

Modelling clay

A small bowl

Some water

Plaster of Paris

Tree bark (or another interesting shape)

How to do it

Press the modelling clay on to the bark and carefully peel it off again. You will find the pattern of the bark in the clay. This is like a mould. Now mix up some Plaster of Paris with water and pour it into your mould. When the Plaster of Paris sets, it will look like the tree bark pattern.

How bottles are made

Plastic bottles are made inside moulds like the one in the picture. The mould is made to look like the outside of the bottle. Bottle moulds are often made in two halves, so a mould can be opened to take out the bottle. If soft plastic is blown up in the mould and then allowed to cool, it takes on the shape of the mould. This is called blow moulding.

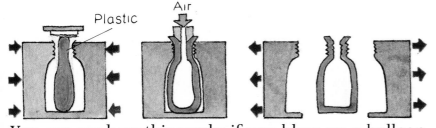

You can see how this works if you blow up a balloon inside a flower pot. As the balloon swells, it takes on the shape of the pot. It fits the sides so closely that you can lift the pot just by holding the end of the balloon.

How buckets are made

Plastic buckets are made by squeezing, or injecting, the soft plastic into a mould through a narrow tube. This is called injection moulding.

Buckets and washing-up bowls are made this way. Look on the bottom of a bucket or bowl. In the middle you may see a small bump where the plastic has been cut from the end of the tube that squirted it into the mould. In the photograph, can you see this bump?

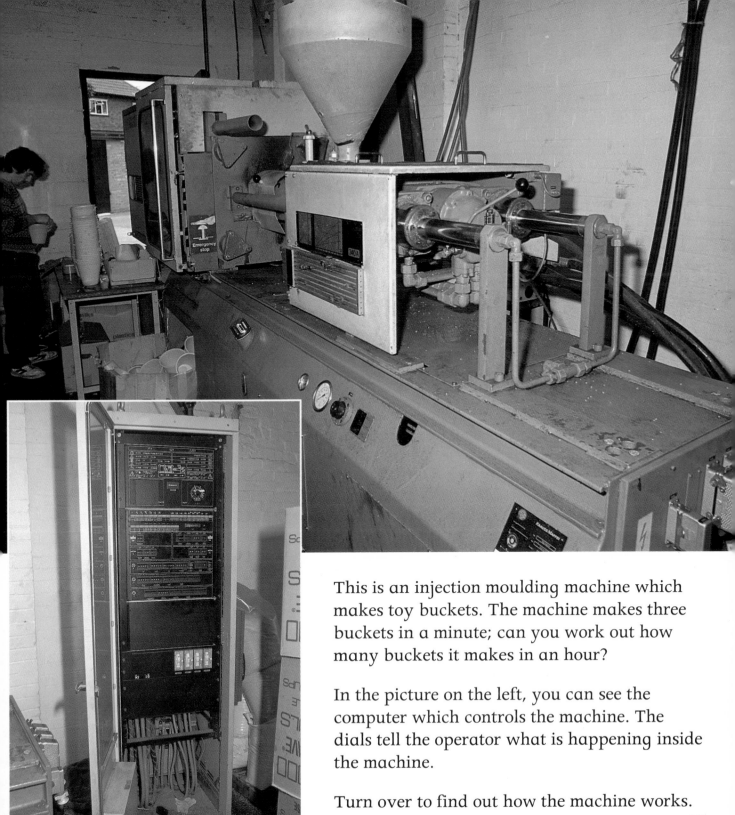

This is an injection moulding machine which makes toy buckets. The machine makes three buckets in a minute; can you work out how many buckets it makes in an hour?

In the picture on the left, you can see the computer which controls the machine. The dials tell the operator what is happening inside the machine.

Turn over to find out how the machine works.

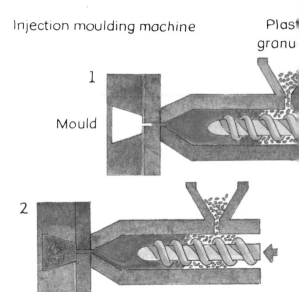

Injection moulding machine

Plast granu

1

Mould

2

In the drawings, you can see what an injection moulding machine looks like inside. The photographs show what it looks like from the outside.

1. First, plastic granules are fed into the machine through a big funnel. Inside the machine, the granules are heated until they melt.

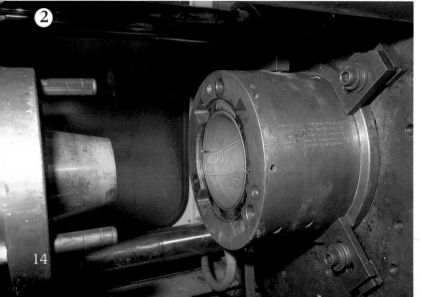

2. In the photograph can you see the marks inside the mould? These marks make the patterns on the sides of the bucket. The liquid plastic is pushed (injected) into the mould.

Ice-cold water around the mould cools the plastic so it sets in the shape of a bucket. When the plastic is cool, the mould opens and the bucket falls out of the machine.

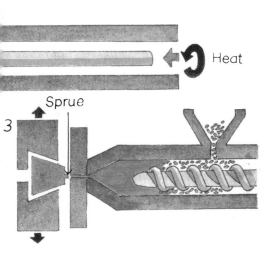

Heat

Sprue

3

Sprue

3. When the bucket comes out of the machine, it has a stalk called a sprue joined to the bottom. This is the plastic that was in the narrow tube which squirted plastic into the mould. On the front cover of this book you can see lots of these sprues.

4. This man's job is to cut the sprues off the bottom of the buckets.

Finally, handles have to be put on the buckets. The finished buckets are then packed in boxes and taken to the shops by lorry.

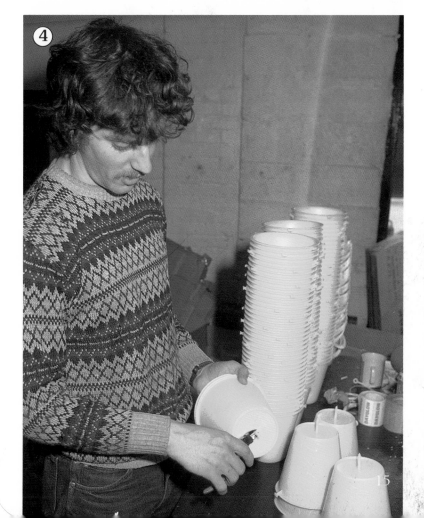

New plastics from old

In the toy factory, the sprues and other waste plastic can be used again. First the waste plastic is sorted into different colours and types. Then it is put into a machine like this one.

Inside the machine, these sharp steel blades chop up the plastic into small pieces.

The pieces of old plastic are mixed with new plastic granules and used to make more toys.

How egg boxes are made

Shapes such as an egg box or the inside of a chocolate box are made by sucking a sheet of warm, soft plastic inside a mould, like this.

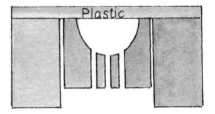

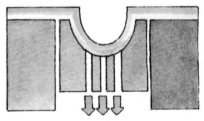

When the plastic cools, it takes on the shape of the mould. This is called vacuum forming.

Look in a mirror and, with your lips tight shut, suck in hard. You will see that your cheeks are pulled in against your jaws in the same way as the plastic sheet is sucked inside the mould.

How pipes and tubes are made

Pipes, rails and tubes are made by squeezing hot plastic through small holes. You can see how this is done if you squeeze icing out of the end of an icing bag. (Ask an adult to help you make the icing.)

Try squeezing the icing through different shaped nozzles. What shapes do you get? Can you match up these shapes with the right nozzles?

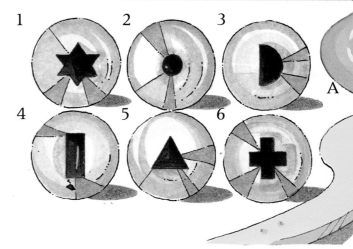

18

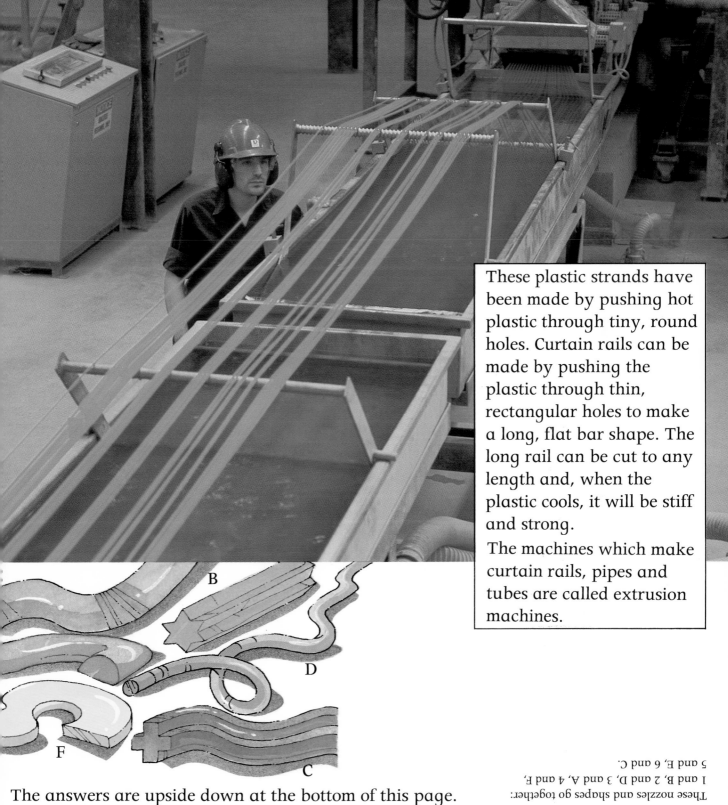

These plastic strands have been made by pushing hot plastic through tiny, round holes. Curtain rails can be made by pushing the plastic through thin, rectangular holes to make a long, flat bar shape. The long rail can be cut to any length and, when the plastic cools, it will be stiff and strong.

The machines which make curtain rails, pipes and tubes are called extrusion machines.

The answers are upside down at the bottom of this page.

These nozzles and shapes go together:
1 and B, 2 and D, 3 and A, 4 and F,
5 and E, 6 and C.

19

Plastics for clothes

Some special plastics can be squeezed through tiny holes so they come out as fine, strong threads. These threads can be woven into material for clothes.
Look at the labels inside your clothes. Can you find any labels that say nylon or polyester? These are plastics.

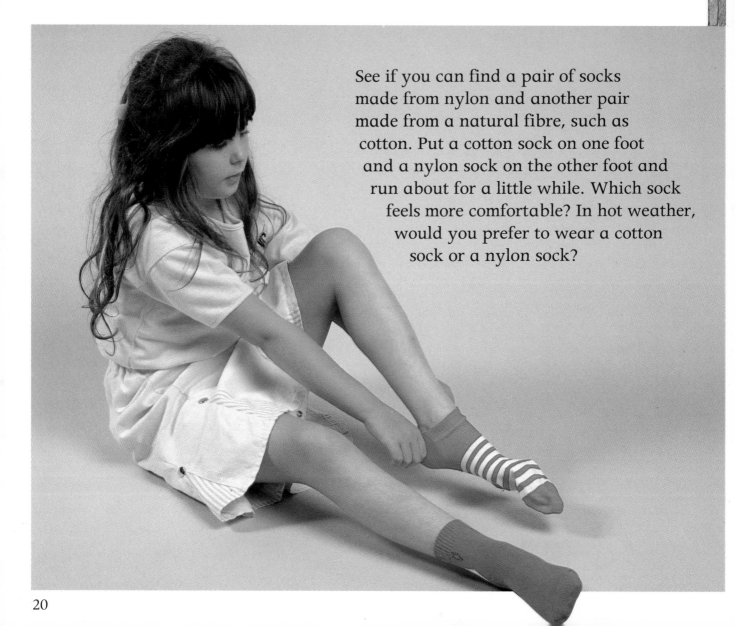

See if you can find a pair of socks made from nylon and another pair made from a natural fibre, such as cotton. Put a cotton sock on one foot and a nylon sock on the other foot and run about for a little while. Which sock feels more comfortable? In hot weather, would you prefer to wear a cotton sock or a nylon sock?

How strong are plastics?

Have you ever helped to carry the shopping
and found that the handle of the bag has snapped
or the bottom of the bag has torn? Are plastic bags
stronger than paper ones? Can you think of a fair
test to find the strongest carrier bag?

Do plastics keep things warm?

Materials which keep warm things warm (and cold things cold) are called insulators. Try this test to see if plastics are better insulators than natural materials.

You will need

Something made from cotton

Elastic bands

Something made from polyester

A piece of polystyrene (ceiling tiles and packing materials are often made from this)

5 plastic cups (make sure they are all the same size and shape)

Lots of ice cubes

Something made from wool

How to do it

1. Put the same number of ice cubes into each cup. Wrap one cup in wool, one in cotton, one in polyester and one in polystyrene. Use the elastic bands to hold the materials around the cups.

It doesn't matter what order you do this in as long as you leave one cup open and unwrapped.

22

2. When the ice in the open cup has melted, undo the other cups. What do you think you will find? Do you think that the cloth has warmed the ice and melted it? Or have you discovered that it stops the cold from escaping and keeps the ice solid? Which material keeps the ice solid for longest? This one is the best insulator.

Plastics and the environment

If you tried the tests to compare plastic bags with paper bags, you may have found that paper bags fall apart much more easily than plastic ones. But the strength of plastic bags is not always a good thing.

Bury some plastic objects in the ground next to some paper and cardboard. Mark the spot. After a few weeks, dig everything up again. You will find that the paper and card is beginning to rot away, but the plastic is as good as new. Plastic rubbish is very hard to get rid of. This is one reason why scientists are trying to make more plastics that will break up and rot away.

Plastics are very useful because they can be made into so many different products and they last a long time. But what will happen to all the plastic rubbish you throw away every day?

More things to do

1. Which are the best materials to wear in the rain? Can you think of a clever way of testing clothes to see how water-proof they are? Once they are wet right through, which materials dry the fastest, man-made plastic materials, such as nylon, or natural ones like wool or cotton?

2. Which do you think are the most comfortable pillows, those filled with feathers or those filled with plastic foam? Do a survey to find out what the rest of your class thinks when they try the two different kinds of pillows.

3. Expanded polystyrene is the name of the plastic that meat trays and ceiling tiles are made from. It is very light and floats well. How much weight can a small piece hold before it sinks? Does it float better than wood? Does it float higher in water than cork?

4. Some wall-paper has a thin plastic coat, called vinyl. If it gets dirty you can wipe it clean with a damp cloth. This can be helpful, but why will it be a problem when you need to strip the wall to put up new paper?

5. Make a list of things which were once made from glass and are now made from plastic. Which do you think is better, plastic or glass? Why? What other materials has plastic replaced?

6. Plastic bottles have to take quite a battering when they get bumped, dropped and banged. Can you think of a way of testing different bottles to see which ones are the strongest?

7. Imagine a world without plastics. What natural things could you use instead? Shoes were once made from leather – now many of them are plastic. Do plastic shoes last longer than leather ones? How could you find out?

8. Are eggs better protected in cardboard egg boxes or plastic ones?

9. Try rubbing something plastic, such as a comb, plastic pen or bottle, against your jumper. Then hold the object near your hair. What happens? Find out what happens after 10 rubs and after 20 rubs. Does this happen with objects made from wood, paper or other materials?

Index

(Numbers in **bold** type are pages which show activities.)

blow moulding **11**

cloth 5, **20**, **22**
computer 13
cooling 14
curtain rails 18, 19

dye 8

egg boxes 17
extrusion machine 19

granules 8, 14, 16

hard plastic 5, 6
heating 8, 9, 10, 11, 12, 14, 17, 18, 19
injection moulding 12–15
insulator **22–23**

making plastic 8
moulding 10, **11**, 12–15, 17

nylon 5, 8, 20

oil-based plastics 8

pipes 18
polyester 20
polystyrene 25
polythene 8
plastic bags 8, 9
plastic bottles 8, 11
plastic buckets 12–15
plastic rubbish 24

re-cycled plastic 16

scientists 24
shaping 8, 9, **10**, 11, 12, 13, 14, 15, 16, 17, 18, 19, 20
sprue 15, 16
squeezing **18**, 19, 20

testing **6–7**, **20**, 21, **25**
tubes 18

vacuum forming **17**

waste plastic 16, 24